About This Book

Title: *On the Farm*

Step: 6

Word Count: 257

Skills in Focus: Vowel-r combination ar

Tricky Words: animals, through, money, protects, into, people, small, fruit

Ideas For Using This Book

Before Reading:
- **Comprehension:** Look at the title and cover image together. Walk through the pictures in the book with readers and have them make predictions about what they might learn while reading. Help them make connections by asking what they already know about farms.
- **Accuracy:** Practice saying the tricky words listed on page 1.
- **Phonics:** Tell students they will read words with the spelling *ar*. Write the letter combination on a piece of paper. Have students look at the word *farm* in the title on the front cover. Ask readers to point to the letters in the word that say /ar/. Write *farm* on the piece of paper, underlining the letters that represent the target sound. Repeat with the story words *start, harvest, parts, barn, garden,* and *hard*. Have readers look through the first few pages to see if they can find any other examples of words that have the letter combination *ar*.

During Reading:
- Have readers point under each word as they read it.
- **Decoding:** If readers are stuck on a word, help them say each sound and blend the sounds together smoothly. Be sure to point out words with the *ar* spelling as they appear.
- **Comprehension:** Invite readers to talk about new things they are learning about farms while reading. What are they learning that they didn't know before?

After Reading:
Discuss the book. Some ideas for questions:
- Have you ever been to a farm before? What plants and animals did you see there?
- What other types of farm animals and plants do you know?

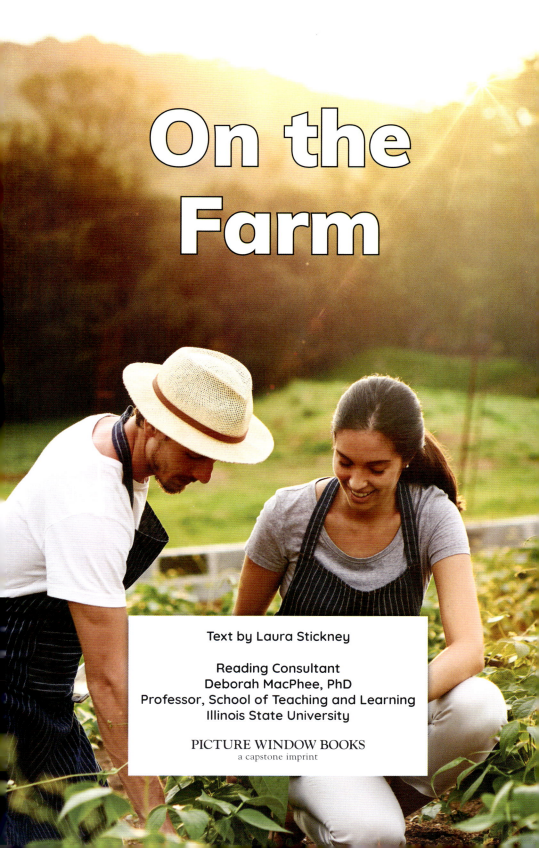

On the Farm

Text by Laura Stickney

Reading Consultant
Deborah MacPhee, PhD
Professor, School of Teaching and Learning
Illinois State University

PICTURE WINDOW BOOKS
a capstone imprint

Farms are places where people harvest plants and raise animals.

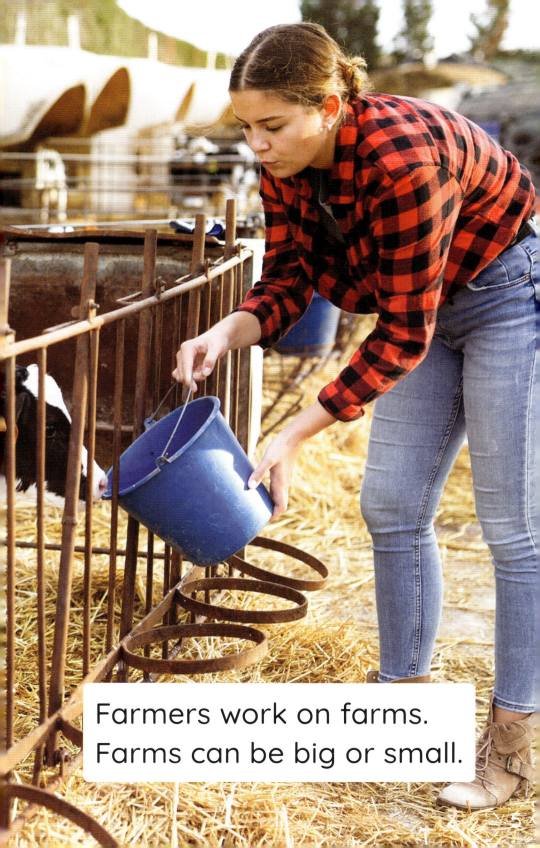

Farmers work on farms. Farms can be big or small.

Farms have many parts. They have barns, yards, and pens.

Farms have big fields and gardens too.

Crops

Farmers get up early to start work. Farmers must care for their plants.

The weather can be hard on crops.

Farmers drive tractors through the fields. They harvest plants like corn, beans, and pumpkins.

Farmers pick fruit from gardens.

Farmers may gather crops in carts.

They pull the carts out of the fields.

Farmers sell part of their harvest to stores. They earn money when they sell the harvest.

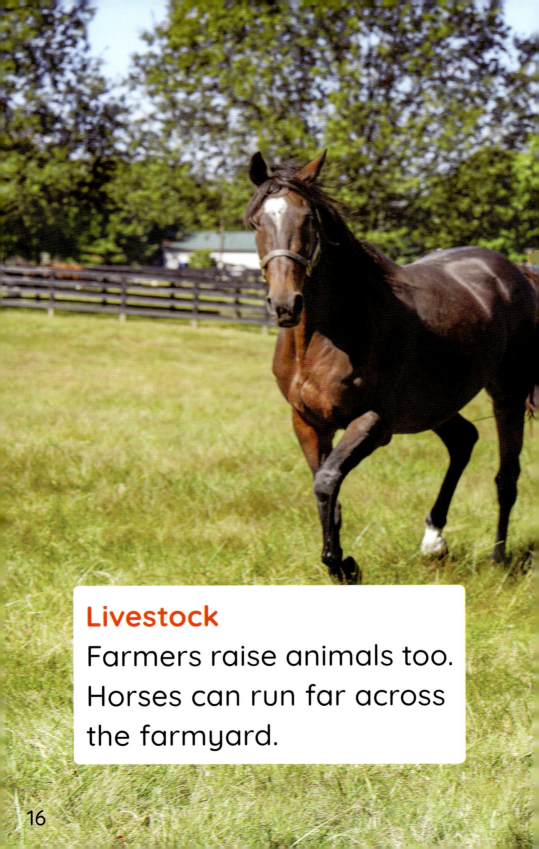

Livestock

Farmers raise animals too. Horses can run far across the farmyard.

Pigs live in pens on the farm.
They have floppy ears.
You can hear pigs snort.
They splash in mud puddles.

They sleep in barn stalls. The barn keeps them warm.

Farmers keep chickens in a coop. It has a bar that locks.

The coop protects chickens from harm when it gets dark. It keeps them warm.

Some animals help farmers do work. Horses pull large carts for farmers.

Dogs herd sheep in the yard.

A farmer milks cows and goats. To start, she uses her hands and arms to squeeze milk into a pail. This is hard work!

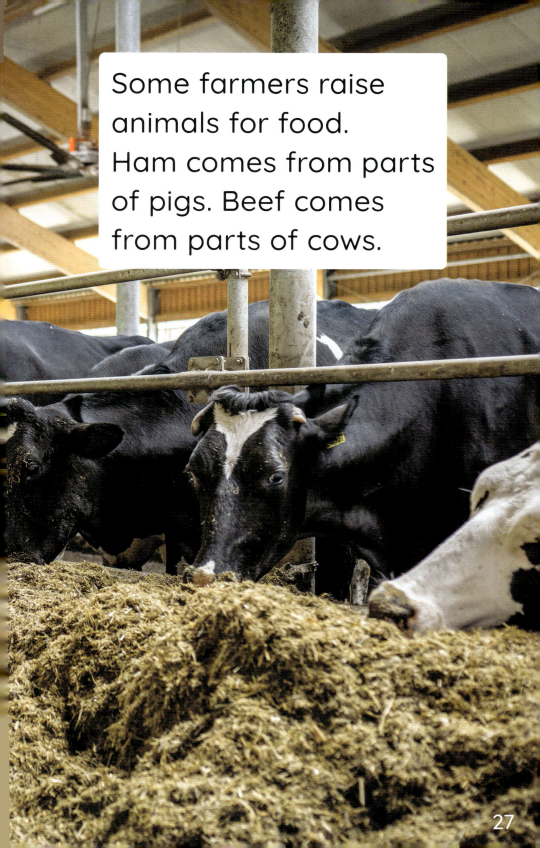

Some farmers raise animals for food. Ham comes from parts of pigs. Beef comes from parts of cows.

Farmers harvest this meat. They take it to market. They earn money when it sells at market.

Farming is hard work!

More Ideas:

Phonics Activity

Writing with *ar* Words:
Ask readers to write a story using as many words as possible that have the *ar* letter combination. The story can be as silly or serious as readers want!

Suggested words: farm, barn, harm, dark, warm, market, hard, garden, part

Extended Learning Activity

What If You Were a Farmer?
Ask readers to imagine that they are farmers working on a farm. Have them think about what kinds of animals and plants they would have on their farm. What work needs to be done on the farm? Have students write a few sentences about their farm. Challenge them to use words with the *ar* letter combination in their sentences.

Published by Picture Window Books, an imprint of Capstone
1710 Roe Crest Drive, North Mankato, Minnesota 56003
capstonepub.com

Copyright © 2026 by Capstone.
All rights reserved. No part of this publication may be reproduced in whole or in part, or stored in a retrieval system, or transmitted in any form or by any means, electronic, mechanical, photocopying, recording, or otherwise, without written permission of the publisher.

Library of Congress Cataloging-in-Publication Data is available on the Library of Congress website.

ISBN: 9798875227257 (hardback)
ISBN: 9798875231346 (paperback)
ISBN: 9798875231322 (eBook PDF)

Image Credits: Getty: Hispanolistic/E+, cover; iStock: AleksandarGeorgiev, 12, Frazao Studio Latino, 14–15, Irina Kononova, 24–25, JuliaLototskaya, 18, liu mingzhu, 11, PeopleImages, 8, ProfessionalStudioImages, 7, sasapanchenko, 20, sergeyryzhov, 28–29, Try Media, 16–17, vm, 26–27, WoodyUpstate, 6; Shutterstock: AZP Worldwide, 9, BearFotos, 4–5, Irina Gust, 13, La Famiglia, 1, 30, Michael Siluk, 21, oticki, 10, 32, PeopleImages.com - Yuri A, 2–3, smereka, 22, The Old Major, 23, YuenSiuTien, 19

Printed and bound in China. 6274